WITH STENDHAL

With Stendhal

~ *Introduction, Translation and Notes by* ~

SIMON LEYS

Published by Black Inc.,
an imprint of Schwartz Media Pty Ltd
Level 5, 289 Flinders Lane
Melbourne Victoria 3000 Australia
email: enquiries@blackincbooks.com
http://www.blackincbooks.com

The National Library of Australia
Cataloguing-in-Publication entry:

With Stendhal / Simon Leys.

ISBN: 9781863954792 (pbk.)

Stendhal, 1783-1842. Stendhal, 1783-1842--Aesthetics.
Art and literature--France--History--19th century.
Aesthetics, French.

Other Authors/Contributors:
Leys, Simon, 1935-

848

Book design: Thomas Deverall
Printed in Australia by Griffin Press

Front cover image: Henri Beyle (Stendhal),
oil portrait by Johan Olaf Sodemark (1840)

To the happy few [†]

---

†   See Page 75, Note 15.

CONTENTS

FOREWORD

Two short texts shed an exceptionally penetrating light on Stendhal's heart: one is *Henri Beyle*,[†] the memoir (once deemed scandalous) that Prosper Mérimée wrote in mourning homage to his friend. The other, *Les Privilèges*, is an enigmatic – yet revealing – fantasy which Stendhal himself improvised on an idle afternoon near the end of his life, purely for his own pleasure.

Though Stendhal does not lack passionate admirers in the English-speaking world, it appears that neither of these two illuminating documents has ever been translated into English, which gave me the idea to remedy this strange gap. Still, had such a translation already existed, I doubt if this could have discouraged me from undertaking the present work: who would give up the chance to spend some hours with Stendhal?

S.L.
Canberra, September 2009

[†] Originally titled *H.B.* – a title often retained in modern editions.

PART I: Stendhal according to Mérimée

INTRODUCTION

Albert Thibaudet (1874–1936) – who was a remarkable critic – drew an interesting distinction between writers who "have a position" (think of Victor Hugo, for instance) and writers who "have a presence" (here the example of Stendhal immediately comes to mind).

We feel captivated, inspired, overwhelmed when we read *Les Misérables*, without necessarily experiencing a particular urge to explore Hugo's life; or, should we do this, the exercise would probably not significantly increase our appreciation of his masterpiece – it might even dampen our admiration, as we discover that the author was rather less magnanimous than his creation.

With Stendhal, the reverse is true. Beylists (interestingly enough, admirers of Hugo do not call themselves Hugolians) devour with passion every scrap of paper on which Henri Beyle has scribbled something – in fact, some of his most original ideas, witticisms and paradoxes were scattered in utterly haphazard fashion: jotted down in the margins of books, on loose sheets or on the back of used envelopes. We read all these with equal eagerness, in the hope of achieving an ever

3

more intimate understanding of the man behind the writing.

In the conclusion of his essay on Stendhal, Paul Valéry grasped the heart of the matter: "Henri Beyle, in my view, represents a certain type of mind, much more than he ever was a 'man of letters'. And this is also the reason why people like or dislike him – and why I love him. We shall never be done with Stendhal. I can think of no greater praise than that."

*

Beylists are ambivalent towards Mérimée's brief memoir. They treasure it – and it shocks them.

They treasure it, for it is a vivid record of impressions and psychological insights, first-hand information, *logia* and anecdotes written by a privileged witness – a shrewd observer, good writer and close friend – who knew Stendhal during the last twenty years of his life.

The friendship between the two men was genuine, but it was also fraught with one difficulty, which came to cast an increasing shadow over their otherwise delightful exchanges. When they first met, Mérimée was still in his twenties, while Stendhal was twice his age. Quite early, Mérimée developed a very successful career, both on the literary scene (he would eventually be elected to the prestigious Académie Française when he was merely forty-one) and in the civil service, where he reached the position of Inspecteur général des Monuments historiques (an office which he discharged with outstanding competence and distinction). In terms of literary fame and social importance, the younger man soon occupied a position of natural seniority. In contrast, Beyle, whose professional career was erratic, amateurish and chequered, and whose writings were for the most part unfinished, unpublished or unappreciated, offers the image of an eccentric bohemian – an endearing and colourful failure: *un raté*. What irritates modern admirers of Stendhal is the patronising tone which, quite unconsciously, Mérimée often adopted towards him. (In the end, this attitude began to bother Beyle himself: in a private note, he complained of his young friend's vanity, nicknaming him "Academus".) Concerning Stendhal's writings, Mérimée has nothing to say; he merely suggests that he wrote badly and that *De l'Amour* was perhaps not as absurd as it originally appeared. Obviously, it never entered Mérimée's mind – even for one second – that there could come a day when Stendhal's literary fame would totally eclipse his own. The portrait he draws of his dead friend is both affectionate and sharp; nothing escaped his observant eye. He only missed the essential thing: Stendhal's genius. But it would be naïve and unfair to blame him for such a failure, which probably reflects a sort of natural law. A thousand years ago, a great Chinese poet had an intuition of this, as he was passing through the mountain range that surrounds the sublime Mount Lu:

> I never saw the true face of Mount Lu
> For the simple reason that I was in the very midst
>   of it.[†]

[†] 不識廬山真面目只緣身在此山中
　　　　　　　　　　　　蘇軾

HENRI BEYLE (STENDHAL)
– Notes & Memories –

Prosper Mérimée

There is a passage in *The Odyssey* that I often recall. The ghost of Elpenor appears to Ulysses and asks for funeral honours:

> μή μ' ἄκλαυτον ἄθαπτον ἰὼν ὄπιθεν καταλείπειν
> "Do not leave me unmourned, unburied"

Nowadays no one is left without a burial, thanks to police regulations. Yet we pagans too have obligations towards our dead that go beyond the requirements of public garbage-disposal. I have attended three pagan funerals. The burial of Sautelet,[1] who had blown his brains out; his mentor, the great philosopher Victor Cousin, and his friends were afraid of bourgeois disapproval and dared not speak a word. There was the burial of Mr Jacquemont,[2] who had forbidden all speeches. And finally, the burial of Beyle. We were three to attend, but were so ill-prepared we did not even know his final wishes. Each time, I felt as if we had been remiss in our duties, if not to the deceased, then at least to ourselves. Should any of our friends die during a journey abroad, we should bitterly regret not having farewelled him at the time of his departure. Departure and death should be surrounded with ceremony, for these are circumstances of some solemnity. At least a meal together, a formal recollection of thoughts – *something* ought to be done. This 'something' is what Elpenor requested: what he demanded was not merely a handful of earth; it was also some sort of memorial.

I am writing the following pages in order to make up for what we failed to do at Beyle's funeral. I wish to share with some of his friends my impressions and memories of him.

Beyle, who was original in all matters – a rare achievement in this age of greyness and timidity – prided himself on his liberal ideas[3] but was, in fact, to the bottom of his soul an utter aristocrat.[4] He could not suffer fools; he had a furious hatred of all boring people, and he never clearly perceived the difference between an evil man and a bore. He expressed a deep contempt for the French character and eloquently denounced the defects attributed – wrongly no doubt – to our great nation: frivolity, thoughtlessness, inconsistency in words and in deeds. And yet he himself displayed these very same defects to a high degree. As regards thoughtlessness, for instance, he once wrote a letter in secret code to Mr de Broglie, the Minister of Foreign Affairs, from Civita Vecchia – and enclosed the key to the code in the same envelope.

Throughout his life, he was entirely ruled by his imagination; he never undertook anything except under the spur of a sudden enthusiasm. And yet he claimed that his actions were always in conformity with reason. "In everything, one must take LO-GIC as one's guide," he used to say, detaching the two syllables of the word. But he had no patience for other people's logic whenever it did not agree with his own. Yet he seldom argued. Those who did not know him well mistook for excessive pride what was perhaps simply his respect for other people's opinions: "You are a cat; I am a rat," was his usual way of closing a discussion.

In 1813, Beyle unwittingly witnessed the rout of an entire brigade, which had been suddenly attacked by a charge of five hundred Cossacks. Beyle saw some two thousand men – including five generals with their embroidered hats – all running for their lives. He ran too, though clumsily, for he was wearing only one boot and carried the other in his hand. On the French side, only two heroes stood their ground against the Cossacks: a gendarme named Menneval, and a conscript who, trying to shoot at the Cossacks, succeeded only in killing the gendarme's horse. Beyle had to report this episode of panic to the Emperor, who listened in mute fury while twirling one of those cast-iron handles that are used for rolling up shutters. Efforts were made to find the gendarme in order to decorate him for his bravery, but he went into hiding and at first attempted to deny having taken any part in the affair; he was convinced that nothing could be worse than attracting attention to oneself in a rout, and thought that the Emperor wanted to have him shot.

On the subject of love,[5] Beyle was more eloquent than on the subject of war. Whenever I met him, he happened to be in love – or at least believed he was. Actually, twice in his life he had great passions from which he never managed to recover. The first one (I think) was inspired by Madam C—, whose beauty was then dazzling. He had many powerful rivals, one of them being General Caulaincourt who, at the time, was at the height of his career.[6] One day, Caulaincourt abused his position and forced Beyle to give way to him in his approach to the lady in question. Beyle immediately composed a short fable, using this allegoric form to challenge the general to a duel, and had it delivered to him that very night. I do not know whether the general understood the fable; at any rate, he ignored its implication, and Beyle received a strong dressing-down from Mr Daru, his relative and patron. Nevertheless, he kept on chasing the lady.

It always seemed to me that Beyle deeply believed in the notion – quite prevalent at the time of the Empire – that any woman can be conquered by storm, and that it is a duty for every man to make the attempt. "Have her; that is your first obligation to her,"[7] he used to tell me whenever he heard that I was in love with a lady.

I never met any man who could accept criticism of his literary works with more equanimity. His friends always used the bluntest language with him: quite often, he sent me manuscripts that he had previously submitted to Victor Jacquemont; they would contain scribbled comments such as: "Detestable – written by a concierge!" and so on. When he published his book *De l'Amour*, they all laughed (quite unfairly, in the end). These criticisms never affected his friendships.

He wrote a great deal and put much work into his books, but instead of polishing their style, he was always modifying their structure. When he erased mistakes from a first draft, he would replace them with new ones, for – as far as I know – he never attempted to improve his expression. No matter how heavily rewritten his manuscripts were, they retained the character of a first draft.[8]

His letters were delightful; reading them was like listening to his conversation.

He was very merry in society – sometimes quite crazy, too often ignoring good manners and tactfulness.[9] Sometimes he could be tasteless, but he was always witty and original. Though he himself was quite blunt, he was easily wounded by innocent reactions. As he told me: "I am a young dog who plays and gets bitten." What he did not appreciate was that he too could also bite sometimes, and quite hard. In fact, he could not understand that others might differ from him in their views and judgements. For instance, in his eyes *all* priests and monarchists had to be hypocrites, by definition.

His opinions on the arts and on literature sounded like bold heresies when he first expressed them. He provoked a storm when he placed Mozart, Cimarosa and

Rossini above the opera-makers of our youth; he was accused, at the time, of having no 'French feelings'.

And yet he is very French when he talks about painting – even though he thinks he sees it from an Italian perspective. He judges the masters according to French criteria, that is, from a literary point of view. He analyzes Italian paintings as if they were dramas. This is the approach that is still cultivated in France, where people have neither feeling for form nor innate taste for colour. It takes a peculiar sensitivity and long practice to love and appreciate form and colour. Beyle endows a Virgin by Raphael with dramatic passions. I always suspected that if he loved the great painters of the Florentine and Lombard schools, it was because their works inspired in him thoughts that probably never crossed their minds. The French, typically, must always judge everything on intellectual grounds. Yet, in all fairness, one should add that no language can account for the subtleties of form or the diverse effects of colour. As one cannot express what one feels, one describes other feelings that everyone can understand.

He rated Canova's sculpture above all others – even Greek sculpture. Perhaps this was because Canova worked for a literary public and was primarily concerned with inspiring ideas in cultivated minds, rather than impressing those with an eye for form.

Imperial police reached everywhere – at least that is what was commonly believed – and Fouché was well aware of what people were saying. Beyle earnestly believed that this gigantic spy-network had retained all its occult power. He gave code-names to his friends and would never call them otherwise. No one knew exactly whom he met, what books he had written, where he had travelled.

I imagine that, in the twentieth century, some critic will discover the writings of Beyle among the hetero-clite mass of books produced in the nineteenth, and will give them the recognition that was denied them in our time. This is how the fame of Diderot eventually grew in the nineteenth century; this is how Shake-speare, forgotten in the time of Saint-Évremond, was discovered by Garrick. One would especially wish that the letters of Beyle be published one day; then readers would learn to know and love a man whose wit and excellent qualities survive now only in the memory of a small number of friends.

I first met Beyle around 1820;[10] from that time until his death, our difference of age notwithstanding,[11] we maintained a close and constant relationship. There are few men whom I have loved more; no other friendship was ever more precious to me.[12] Except for some literary likes and dislikes, we had perhaps not a single idea in common, and there were few subjects on which we found ourselves in agreement. We spent all our time arguing together, each one in complete good faith, yet each one suspecting the other of pig-headedness and love of paradox. We remained good friends nevertheless, and were always delighted to start a new discussion.

For a while, I had suspected his originality to be contrived. Eventually I realized that it was perfectly genuine. Today, examining my memories, I am convinced that his eccentricities were utterly spontaneous; his paradoxes were merely a product of the exaggeration that develops progressively when one cultivates contradiction. Alceste is perfectly genuine when, pressed to apologize for the excessive severity with which he had criticized Oronte's verses, he exclaims in good faith, "A man who writes such verses ought to be hanged!"[13] Beyle's sallies were only, I think, the exaggerated expression of a deep conviction.

I never understood how he developed his unfortunate habit of expressing opinions that contradicted the views of nearly everyone else. What I learned regarding his early education boils down to a single fact: at a very young age, he was entrusted to the care of an old and gloomy priest, whose severity left him with an indelible resentment. To tell the truth, Beyle's spirit rebelled against any form of constraint, including all authority. One could seduce him – this was easy enough – so long as one could amuse him; but it was impossible to impose any opinion upon him, for whoever attempted to exert the slightest pressure on him cut him to the quick. He recalled with bitterness, forty years after the event, how one day, having torn his new clothes at play, he received a scathing reprimand in front of his schoolmates from the priest in charge of his education, who told him that "he brought shame upon his religion and upon his family." This is an example of the tendency to exaggerate mentioned earlier. We were all laughing as Beyle told us the story, but he did not laugh; he saw there an instance of clerical tyranny, a hideous injustice – and this was no joke at all. The wound inflicted on his childish self-respect was still burning him, as on the first day.

"Our parents and our teachers," he said, "are our natural enemies from the day we come into this world." This was one of his aphorisms. As you may well guess, he did not inherit any of his beliefs from his teachers. He often quoted Helvétius with great admiration, and he even forced me to read the treatise *De l'Esprit*;[14] yet he never yielded to my request to re-read it himself. I guess it is there that he picked up some of his ideas, among them the notion that all human intelligences are equal. At least, he could never accept that what seemed wrong to him might appear true to someone else. He believed – in all good faith, I suppose – that in actual fact everyone shared his ideas, and if they expressed them differently it was simply out of self-interest, affectation, fashion or stubbornness. He was resolutely blasphemous, outrageously materialist, or – to put it better – he took divine Providence as his own personal enemy, perhaps in application of the maxim I mentioned earlier. He denied the existence of God, and nevertheless resented him personally, as he did all other authorities. Never could he accept that a religious person may be sincere. I think that his long stay in Italy played an important part in the virulent irreligiosity that is expressed in all his writing, to the great distaste of many readers.

Mr Sainte-Beuve, who is always very perceptive, detected one of the most striking features of Beyle's character: his fear of becoming a dupe and his constant obsession with avoiding such a misfortune. Hence his

contrived cynicism, his obstinate wish to find vile moti-
vations behind any generous deed, his refusal to follow
the spontaneous impulses of his heart – an attitude
which, in his case, (I think) went against his nature.
He hated and despised any false display of sensitivity,
which led him to exaggerate in the opposite direction
– and this, in turn, shocked those who had no intimate knowledge of his character and led them to take
what he said about himself literally. Yet he did not
mind such misunderstandings; not only he did not
bother to rectify the mistaken or sometimes nasty
interpretations that people attached to his words or
his writing, but he took a perverse pleasure (out of
vanity, I guess) in appearing, in the eyes of the public,
as a monster of immorality. As he said in one of his
prefaces (I don't recall which one): "I write only for
some twenty readers whom I have never met, but who
understand me – maybe ..."[15]

In his eyes, there were only two sorts of people in
this world: those he found amusing and those he
found boring. In order to win the consideration or the
affection of the latter, he would have deemed it an
unbearable obligation to make the slightest sacrifice or
the slightest effort. Beyle's independent spirit, or (one
may say) his wandering impulse, rejected any form of

constraint. Whatever impeded his freedom was odious to him, and I am not sure if he ever clearly appreciated the difference between a man who was simply boring and a man who was downright wicked. His constant desire to fathom all the mysteries of the human heart sometimes induced him to keep company with people for whom he had little respect. "Yet," he said, "with them I might at least learn something." Besides, his noble and loyal spirit and his unbending integrity made him abandon such company as soon as it offered him advantages other than the mere satisfaction of his curiosity.

His views on men and affairs were essentially influenced by the memory of the boredom or the pleasure they had given him. He could not tolerate boredom and agreed with the medical doctor who authorized the Duke of Lauraguais to launch a criminal action against an utter bore for attempted manslaughter. He would dream up the most extravagant punishments for men or books that had the misfortune of making him yawn.

Beyle was essentially imaginative and impulsive, and yet he insisted he must find a reason for everything and behave, in all circumstances, according to the rules of logic. The word cropped up often in his conversation, and his friends recall the particular emphasis with which he slowly pronounced it, detaching the two syllables as if they were separated by a comma: LO, GIC. Logic ought to guide us in all our undertakings, but his logic was quite peculiar and his line of reasoning sometimes hard to grasp. I remember him asking one day as we were toying with the idea of writing a drama together whose hero, guilty of a crime, is tormented by remorse: "In order to liberate oneself from remorse, what would LO-GIC advise?" He reflected for an instant. "We should establish a School for Mutual Enlightenment." Our drama did not develop any further.

He said that at the start of his life a man should have a store of ready-made maxims with which to confront all the most common misfortunes. Once adopted, these maxims should never be modified; when in doubt before any situation, the only question was how to identify quickly which maxim should be applied. *Never forgive a lie. When first entering society, grab the first opportunity to challenge someone to a duel. Never regret something silly you did or said.* Such were some of his maxims.[16]

Though he was never particularly daring with women, he encouraged young men to be bold: "You will succeed one time out of ten. Or, let us say, one time out of twenty; but this possibility of being lucky once, is it not worth the risk of nineteen rebuffs, the risk of being nineteen times ridiculous?"

He laughed at me, as I was studying Greek when I was twenty. He said: "You are on the battlefield; this is no longer the time to polish your gun. You must shoot!"

After his maxims came his tips, which he offered with guarantees of success. I still remember a few. One of the main causes of torment is false shame. For a young man, entering a drawing room is a big affair. He thinks everyone is looking at him, and he is dying of fear: is my appearance absolutely impeccable? One of our friends suffered more acutely than most from such shyness; Beyle used to say that when he saw our friend enter Madam Pasta's drawing room, he would look as if he had broken the china in the antechamber. "I'll give you an old tip of mine," Beyle told him. "Walk in with exactly the same attitude as you happened perchance to have while still on the stairs – whether appropriate or not, never mind. Be like the statue of the Commander, and do not change your demeanour until your initial stage fright has completely disappeared."

Here is his tip for a first duel:[17] while your opponent is taking aim at you, look at a tree and apply yourself to counting its leaves. Concentrating the mind on one thing will help you not to worry about the other matter – the more serious one. When it is your turn to aim at your opponent, recite two Latin verses; this will prevent you from shooting too soon and will counteract the excessive emotion that usually sends the shot twenty feet above its target.

"If you find yourself alone with a woman, I give you five minutes to prepare yourself for the formidable effort of telling her, 'I love you.' Tell yourself: 'I am a coward if I do not tell her within the next five minutes.' It does not matter how you make your declaration; the main thing is to find a way to break the ice, and to be totally determined to despise yourself should your courage fail."

Beyle preached "sensible love", but he was quite subject to blind passion. There was a certain lady whose name he could not pronounce without keeping his voice from faltering. In 1836 I saw him again after a long absence. We arranged to meet some sixty miles out of Paris; we had a thousand things to tell each other. We chatted the whole evening, walking to and fro on the public promenade of a small town.[18] (Are there any places in France where one can find greater solitude?) There he told me, with deep emotion, the story of this love. It is the only time I ever saw him cry. Their very long affection for one another was no longer shared: his mistress had become reasonable, whereas he remained as crazy as he had been at twenty. "How can you still be in love with me?" she asked him. "I am forty-five." "To me," Beyle said, "she is still the same age as when we first made love together." He foresaw the end of an affair that was dearer to him than ever. The unique prospect towards which all his emotions had been directed was about to be annihilated. He recalled the past audacities of this woman, who had sadly now become so cautious, and was carried away by these memories. But then, with the sharp observer's eye that never left him, he would detail all the tiny symptoms that betrayed her increasing indifference. LO-GIC was not forgotten. "After all, her behaviour is quite reasonable. She used to enjoy playing whist; now she does not like it any more. I still like to play whist – too bad for me. She is from a country where falling into ridicule is deemed to be the worst misfortune. To be still in love at her age is ridiculous. For the last eighteen months she has taken that dreadful risk for my sake. For me, these were eighteen months of stolen bliss."[19] And we debated at length the truth of these verses of Dante:

Nessun maggior dolore
Che ricordarsi del tempo felice
Nella miseria.†

He maintained that Dante was wrong, and that memories of happy times remain always and everywhere a form of happiness. I remember I was defending the view of the poet. Today, however, it seems to me that Beyle was right.

In Italy he had another love affair, which he did not wish to evoke. Once, however, he told me how this love came to its tragic end. The lady[20] had a husband who was very jealous – at least that is what she said – and she insisted that he always be very cautious. Therefore their meetings had to be few and were always surrounded with utter secrecy. To prevent any suspicion, Beyle was obliged to hide in a small town, some twenty miles from the lady's residence. Whenever he obtained a rendezvous, he would travel *incognito*,

---

† "There is no greater sorrow than to recall a time of happiness in misery." (*The Divine Comedy*, Inferno, I.121)

changing carriages several times to put the spies – who, he thought, were always following him – off his trail; then he would reach his goal in complete darkness, clad in a long cloak, and a trusted chambermaid would usher him into his mistress's apartments. For some time all went well; but eventually the chambermaid, who either bore a grudge against her mistress or was bribed by Beyle, imparted a stunning revelation: the husband was not at all jealous; the wife (notwithstanding the well-known loyalty of all Italian ladies, in contrast to the notorious coquetry of our own women) was demanding such secrecy from Beyle simply to prevent any confrontation between him and her other lover – or lovers, for she had several. The chambermaid offered to provide evidence for what she alleged; Beyle accepted the offer. He came to town one day when the lady was not expecting him. The chambermaid hid him in a small dark closet from which he could see with his own eyes, through a tiny hole in the partition, the betrayal that was being performed three feet away from his hiding place.

"Maybe you think that I rushed at them, knife in hand? Not at all. I found the whole scene hilarious. My only concern was not to burst out laughing, which would have ruined the whole thing. I came out of my dark closet as discreetly as I had entered it, still laughing and enjoying the ridiculous side of the whole adventure; besides, I felt contempt for the lady, and was quite pleased after all to have thus recovered my freedom. I went to eat a sorbet, and I met some people I knew. They were struck by my cheerfulness and told me that I looked like a man happily in love. While eating my sorbet and chatting with them, I still felt an irresistible urge to laugh: the puppets I had watched one hour earlier were still dancing before my eyes. Back home, I slept as usual. The next morning, however, the memory of the dark closet had lost its comic character. I only remembered something ugly, something sad, something dirty. Every day this image became more sad, more vile; every day my misfortune weighed heavier. For the next eighteen months I remained in a daze, incapable of any work; I could not write, I could not talk, I could not think. I felt as if oppressed by an unbearable illness, without understanding clearly my own condition. There is no greater misfortune, for it saps all energy. Afterwards, as I was slowly coming out of this crushing listlessness, I experienced a bizarre curiosity: I had to know all her infidelities. This hurt me atrociously; and yet I felt a sort of physical pleasure as I imagined her enacting her countless betrayals. I took my revenge, very stupidly, using persiflage. She regretted our break-up; she tearfully begged for my forgiveness. In my ridiculous pride, I rejected her with scorn. I still see the scene: she followed me, clutching at my clothes, crawling on her knees across a large gallery. I was a fool not to forgive her then, for she certainly never loved me more than on that day."

Beyle's constant concern was the study of passions. Whenever some country bumpkin asked him what his occupation was, he would solemnly reply: "Observer of the human heart." (One day he gave this answer to a fool, who nearly fainted from fear, thinking it was a euphemism for a police spy.) In every anecdote that shed some light on a corner of the heart, he would always single out what he called *le trait* – the word, the gesture through which passion was revealed. For instance, in his view, "crawling on her knees" would be *le trait* in the anecdote above; according to his habit of drawing several conclusions from his own particular experiences, such a gesture was a characteristic expression of remorse and of passionate love.

To conclude on the topic of love, Beyle believed that there was no possibility of happiness for a man unless he was in love. "Once you are in love, everything becomes beautiful in your eyes. I wish I could be in love with Miss Flore (from the Variétés Theatre) and I would have nothing for which to envy Don Juan."

After love, literature occupied the greatest place in Beyle's heart. He loved reading and wrote all the time. *Nulla dies sine linea*, as he often told me,[21] reproaching my laziness. Even though there are oversights to be found in his writing, he used to work on it at great length. All his books were rewritten several times before being delivered to the printers, but his corrections did not bear upon the style. He always wrote at great speed; he revised only his ideas, and never paid attention to form. He despised all stylistic concerns and maintained that an author has achieved perfection when his readers remember only his ideas without recalling his actual words. He hated preciosity and bombast;[22] he was scathing towards those writers who turn phrases into an elaborate patchwork and try to impress the reader by dressing their banal thoughts in bizarre apparel. He had a sincere and well-informed admiration for our great prose writers of the seventeenth and eighteenth centuries. He was constantly re-reading them in order, he said, to ward off miasmas from current writing fashions.

He was completely deaf to poetry. He often muti-
lated French verses while quoting them. Though he
spoke fluent Italian and had a fairly good knowledge
of English, he had no ear for metre and accent in the
poetry of these two languages. Yet he showed a deep
appreciation of Shakespeare and Dante, whose beauty
is intimately linked to the poetic form. On poetry, he
made one statement (in *De l'Amour*) which sums up
his incomprehension: "Verses were invented to help
memory; retained on the stage, they are the leftovers of
a Barbarian age." He utterly disliked Racine. Around
1820, we mostly reproached Racine for his total
estrangement from real life – what we used to call in
our romantic jargon *la couleur locale*. Actually, Shakespeare – whom we always opposed to Racine – was, in
this respect, far more grossly at fault, a fact we carefully
neglected to mention.

"Yet," Beyle said, "Shakespeare has a much more
profound knowledge of the human heart. There is no
passion or feeling that he did not grasp in its wonderful
truth, with all its nuances. All his characters are fully
alive, with unique individuality, and this puts him
above all other playwrights."

"And what about Molière?" we would ask. "How do
you rank him?"

"Molière is a rascal who did not dare stage *The Courtier* because Louis XIV did not like it."

Beyle wrote many things on the fine arts, a subject on which he developed his own ideas at a time when everyone else accepted without question the most absurd views, so long as they were endorsed by some famous name. One might say that he discovered Rossini and Italian music. Contemporary connoisseurs will recall the attacks he sustained while promoting the composer of *The Barber of Seville* and *Semiramide* in the face of resistance from the regular public at the Opéra Comique. In the early years of the Restoration, the memory of our defeats had exacerbated national pride and every discussion turned into a patriotic issue. To prefer foreign music to French music all but amounted to a betrayal of our country. From a very early age, Beyle set himself above vulgar prejudices, and on this point, perhaps, he sometimes went too far. Today, however, civilization has made much progress and it is difficult to appreciate all the courage that was needed in 1818 to say that an Italian opera could be better than a French one. It is only when we recall the great battles between the Romantics and the Classicists that we begin to understand why Beyle had to cloak some of his artistic judgements in a certain rhetorical caution. However bold and provocative these views may originally have appeared, they are now universally accepted – mere *truisms*, to borrow a favourite expression of the author.

Without being himself a musician, Beyle had a genuine feeling for melody, which he further developed and cultivated during his journeys through Italy and Germany. In music, it seems that he mostly loved and looked for dramatic effect; or perhaps, instead of analysing his own personal impressions, he translated them into dramatic language, the only one he knew or thought his readers might understand.

It was the same thing with the graphic arts. He had a passionate admiration for the great masters of the Roman, Florentine and Lombard schools; he often saw dramatic intentions in their works which (I believe) are not there. When he discovers in a Virgin by Raphael or by Correggio – the artist he praised above all – all sorts of passions, or nuances of passion, which no painting could ever express, one wonders if he really understood the mind and the purpose of these great painters. Yet he tells us, in his own fashion, the emotions he experienced before their works; he describes what he feels without being able to explain what caused these feelings. Had he attempted to write down his impressions of the same painting at various times, he would probably have been surprised to discover how different they were. Like all critics, Beyle was struggling with a difficulty that is perhaps insoluble. Our language – like all other languages, for all I know – cannot describe with accuracy the qualities of a work of art. We have words to distinguish colours, but for every nuance that has a name, how many more are there that our eyes can appreciate but for which our language has no words? The poverty of language becomes even more evident when we deal with forms instead of colours. Even a poorly trained eye can easily identify a faulty outline; whoever examines a small-scale reproduction of the *Venus de Milo* sees immediately that its nose is modern. And yet the difference between the modern nose and the original one can hardly exceed a fraction of a millimetre. Still, which words could characterize such a form, whose beauty depends upon the addition or the subtraction of a fraction of a millimetre? What we perceive so clearly we cannot express "in black on white", as Beyle used to say. Out of the impossibility of accuracy came the need for terms of comparison – which can hardly shed light on such an obscure question. In the arts, it is the dramatic side which we Frenchmen understand best, and it is probably for this reason that Beyle explains beauty in terms of passion. He pretended to be cosmopolitan, and yet his mind and his heart were utterly French.

It seems to me that he appreciated painting more than sculpture. Antique statues appeared to him too devoid of passion: mindless beautiful bodies. Canova was his favourite sculptor; he admired his elegance even though he found it somewhat mannered. Michelangelo impressed him, but I don't think he really liked him. Once, he took me to see his *Moses* on the tomb of Pope Julius II; he merely praised its expression of implacable ferocity.

Beyle did not care much for the great colourist painters. We argued fiercely on this subject. He deeply despised Rubens and all his school; he reproached the Flemish and even the Venetians for the heaviness of their forms and the vulgarity of their expression. Correggio, according to him, had achieved supreme perfection of form together with exquisite atmospheric perspective. For him, Correggio was the most graceful of all painters, and Michelangelo the most poetically awe-inspiring.

Architecture much interested him, but he looked at monuments only from a picturesque point of view, never considering their actual function. He hated all that was ugly or gloomy, two defects for which he constantly reproached our national architecture. I trust I managed to teach him to distinguish a Romanesque church from a Gothic one, and how to look at each of them,[23] but he condemned them both: "Our dark and lugubrious churches were invented by rascal monks who became rich by scaring timid people." Architecture from the Italian Renaissance pleased him for its delightful elegance; but he paid attention only to its graceful details and not to its overall conception. In spite of LO-GIC, he was guided in such matters not by reason but by imagination.

*

Beyle was a cavalry officer for a few months, and then a military commissioner; in the latter role, he participated in several campaigns, including the campaign of Russia in 1812, during which he was assigned to Napoleon's headquarters. We loved to hear him talk about his experiences in the Emperor's entourage. What he told us bore no resemblance to any of the official reports – as we shall see. Naturally courageous, he observed war with curiosity, without losing his cool. He was not indifferent to the huge, epic events he witnessed, but it was the bizarre and grotesque side of war that caught his eye. Besides, he hated all the exaggerations of patriotic vainglory and, in reaction to such bombast, he often went to the opposite extreme. Like Courier, he ruthlessly mocked what was later called *chauvinism* – an attitude which, after all, has its good side, since it can transform a raw recruit into a tough fighter.

He had a prejudice against all military eloquence, against all the sublime words pronounced on the battlefield. "Do you know what true military eloquence is?" he asked us. "I will give you an example. In a particularly savage engagement, as our line was on the verge of collapsing, one of our bravest generals[24] addressed his men in these words: 'Forward, God damn you all! My bum's as round as a plum! My bum's as round as a plum!' The funny thing is that, in a moment of danger, these words sounded like regular encouragement, and it worked: the frontline regrouped and the enemy was repelled. Trust me, in similar circumstances, Caesar and Alexander spoke to their soldiers in no less sublime fashion."

Another example of military eloquence: "After we left Moscow, on the third day of the retreat, we lost our way and, at dusk, found ourselves – we were some fifteen hundred men – separated from the bulk of the army by a strong Russian division. Part of the night was spent in lamentations. Then, eventually, a few more energetic fellows addressed the cowards and managed to galvanize their determination: tomorrow at first light, we shall force our way through the enemy, sword in hand. Don't imagine that they were told, 'Brave soldiers,' et cetera. Not at all. 'You bunch of scoundrels, you'll all be dead by tomorrow because you are too fucking incompetent to pick up your guns and put them to good use!' This heroic speech bore fruit; at daybreak we marched resolutely towards the Russians, whose campfires could still be seen. We approached silently, with fixed bayonets – and we found only an abandoned dog. The Russians had left during the night."

Beyle said that during the retreat he did not suffer too much from hunger; but he could absolutely not recall how he ate or what he ate, except for a piece of tallow, which cost him twenty francs and proved to be a most memorable feast.

When leaving Moscow, he carried with him a volume of Voltaire's *Facéties*, bound in red leather; he had grabbed it from a burning palace. His companions criticized him as he was reading it at night, by the light of a campfire. The deed was questionable: removing a single volume had spoiled a magnificent set! He himself eventually developed a sort of remorse, and a few days later abandoned the volume in the snow.

He was one of the few who, amid all the miseries the army had to suffer during the disastrous retreat from Moscow, managed to retain at all times their moral strength, the respect of their companions and their own self-respect. Once, near the Beresina river, answering the call of his superior, Mr Daru, he arrived clean-shaven and carefully dressed. Mr Daru told him, "You have shaved, Monsieur? You are truly a man."

Mr Bergonié, Commissioner of the Conseil d'Etat, attached to central headquarters, told me that he owed his life to Beyle who, having foreseen the congestion on the bridges over the Beresina, forced him to cross to the other side on the evening before the rout. He practically had to drag him all the way. Bergonié was full of praise for Beyle's self-control and commonsense; these qualities never left him, not even when the bravest were losing their heads. Beyle remained resourceful in dire circumstances; he modestly explained that he owed this advantage to his stock of ready-made maxims: thanks to them, he was ready to act while others were wasting their time in deliberations.

Like many people of his age, Beyle (it seems to me) judged his contemporaries with great severity, whereas he had some indulgence for my generation. He admired the appetite for study and the desire to know things in depth that characterized young men of twenty when he himself was in his forties. Our seriousness amused him, as did our pedantry, but he said that, unlike the youth of his time, we were no dupes. True to his habit of presenting himself as worse than he was, he feigned contempt for the enthusiasm that had enabled men of his generation to achieve so many great things. "We all burned with holy zeal – even I, however unworthy. I was sent to Brunswick in order to raise an extraordinary levy of five million. I managed to raise seven, and was nearly set upon by a rebellious rabble incensed by my excessive energy. The Emperor, however, asked which commissioner had achieved this result and said: 'Well done.'"

It was difficult to know what exactly his feelings were towards Napoleon. He almost always adopted an opinion opposite to the one presented to him. By turns, he was sarcastic or enthusiastic; sometimes he called him a *parvenu* intoxicated by his baubles and devoid of all LO-GIC; at other times he expressed an admiration bordering on idolatry. In succession, he was as impertinent as Courier and as obsequious as Las Cases. The personalities of the Empire received similarly diverse treatment. On one point, however, his view did not vary: all who approached the Emperor became fascinated by him. Beyle started to write a history of Napoleon; a fragment of it, dashed off with verve, was incorporated into the narrative of his journeys through France; it describes the Emperor's arrival in Grenoble, in 1815.[25]

From what Beyle said, it seems that at the time of his youth there was less selfishness than today. Even the modish behaviour had more nobility. For instance, although Beyle himself was fond of good food, he would not admit this fact. He even expressed the opinion that the time we spend on eating is wasted, and wished that it were possible to be rid of hunger for a whole day, simply by swallowing a pill in the morning. Nowadays, people pride themselves on being gourmets. In Beyle's time a man would take pride, first of all, in his energy and his courage. How could you go to war if you were a gastronome?

Beyle was fond of intimate gatherings with a few people. In a small circle of friends and persons with whom he felt in sympathy, he would happily abandon himself to his natural gaiety. He did not try to shine, but merely to have fun and to entertain, "For," he said, "you must pay your entrance ticket."[26] Always amusing, he was sometimes a little crazy, indecent even, but he made people laugh, and it was difficult to resist his mirth in the name of good manners. However, the presence of one boring man, of one unpleasant guest, was enough to make him freeze and quickly run away. He never learned the art of bearing with boredom. He said that life is short and the time lost in yawns is never returned. He was very fond of the observation by Mr de M—: "Bad taste leads to crime."[27]

Good faith characterized Beyle's personality. No one was more loyal or trustworthy. I never met a writer who was more straightforward in expressing his criticism, nor more magnanimous in accepting it from his friends. He enjoyed sharing his manuscripts and invited frank comment; critical observations, however severe – even unfair – never provoked his resentment. One of his maxims was that no one who professionally puts 'black on white' ought be surprised or offended when readers call him a fool. He truly put this maxim into practice, and this did not reflect any indifference on his part – real or feigned. Criticism commanded all his attention; he would discuss it in lively fashion, but without acrimony, and as if discussing the works of an author who had died many centuries ago.

He had adopted the bizarre habit of shrouding his most ordinary activities in secrecy, in order to put the police off his track – as if the police would be naïve enough to bother collecting mundane gossip. All his letters were signed with false names: "César Bombet", "Cotonet" et cetera.[28] They were dated from "Abeille" instead of Civita Vecchia, and often he would start with a phrase such as, "I safely received your delivery of raw silk and have stored it in my warehouse, awaiting shipment." The notes he was constantly jotting down were couched in the form of impenetrable riddles, the meaning of which he himself could not even guess a few days later.

He was not afraid of death, but did not like to talk about it; for him the subject was not frightening, but he considered it unclean and ugly. He died the death he would have chosen,[29] the death Caesar had wished for himself: *Repentinam inopinatamque.*†

---

† an instantaneous and unexpected [death].

APPENDIX I. *Note on Mérimée*

Prosper Mérimée (1803–1870) was born in Paris, into an upper-middle-class family, the only child of two artists. His father had graduated from the prestigious École des Beaux-Arts with the Second Prize for painting (he eventually wrote a huge treatise on the technique of oil painting "from van Eyck to the present-day"); his mother was a portrait painter and taught drawing at the École Polytechnique. Mérimée himself received early artistic training at home and became a competent amateur (later in life, for instance, during a long visit to Spain, he copied a number of works by Velázquez in the Prado); however, following the wishes of his father, he took a degree in law which in turn enabled him to enter the civil service, where his ascent was swift. By age twenty-eight he was promoted to positions of high responsibility and became chief of staff for various ministers (in succession, Navy, Commerce, Interior). Yet, from the start, literature was – and always remained – his great love. He had determined to become a writer and his first publications in his early twenties (short theatrical plays, short stories) at once earned him critical acclaim. His literary output was eventually limited both by the absorbing demands of his official career and by his own exacting standards of perfection, but it was never totally discontinued, nor did it ever flag in quality. His writing, which hardly evolved, is always cool, detached, terse, incisive, with a touch of sardonic humour; it rejects sentimental effusion and self-revelation, and usually hides its deep sensitivity behind a mask of cynicism.

The great turning point in his professional activity came in 1834: he was appointed Inspecteur général des Monuments historiques and placed in charge of all the ancient architectural treasures of the entire country. This fairly new position (it had been created three years earlier, on a visionary initiative of the Prime Minister, François Guizot) was still ill-defined; with no qualifications other than his intelligence, culture (classical and historical) and an affinity for the spatial arts, Mérimée was to occupy the post for the next twenty-six years – with exceptional success. He laid down principles, aims and methods by which to perform a gigantic task (still pursued today): the inventory, protection, preservation, maintenance and restoration of the French monumental heritage. His achievements were simply prodigious – his personal interventions salvaged countless monuments that, through neglect or vandalism, were on the edge of total obliteration. If we can still admire today some of the most sublime creations of medieval civilisation, it is thanks to Mérimée's initiatives; think, for instance, of the basilica of Vézelay, or the stained-glass windows of Chartres, or the wall paintings of Saint-Savin, to mention only three famous examples out of – literally – *hundreds* of rescued treasures.

His workload was crushing; he discharged it with patience and passion, with enthusiasm and scholarly expertise. Every year, he would spend at least three months on the highways and backroads of the entire country, on a systematic inspection of regional France, in order to establish a national inventory of all ancient monuments, assessing each one for its past history and present condition. These journeys were strenuous: communications were slow and difficult, transportation was poor and rough, accommodation in village inns was primitive. In the field, he had to deal with, fight or cajole ignorant clergy, philistine local authorities, looters and vandals. In some instances, to prevent imminent disfigurement or downright destruction of priceless architecture, he had to rush back to Paris, pull strings, get in touch with the Prime Minister, secure his personal intervention, obtain extraordinary credit ... He trained his own team of architects specialized in historical restoration work and, in the end, before taking his retirement, wisely groomed the ablest of them to be his successor.

Alongside his professional activity he led a busy social life: the literary *salons* in Paris, the Académie Française. After the coup d'état through which Louis-Napoléon transformed himself into Emperor Napoléon III, Mérimée (to the dismay of his liberal friends) became part of the inner circle of the imperial court. He was a very old friend of Empress Eugénie, who was still a child when he first met her parents – impoverished aristocrats in Madrid. He had a fatherly affection for her, and she regarded him as a sort of spiritual mentor. Much against Mérimée's own wishes, the Emperor insisted on appointing him a Senator. In frail health, he escaped Parisian honours and obligations as often as possible by spending most of his time on the Côte d'Azur where, in his last years, he resumed his practice of painting (water-colours and gouache).

Having witnessed the national disasters of 1870 and the collapse of the Second Empire, Mérimée died – despairing, sick and broken in spirit. A few days before his death, he wrote to a lady friend:[30] "I have endeavoured all my life to free myself from prejudice and to

be a citizen of the world before being a Frenchman –
but now these philosophical overcoats are of no use.
Today I am bleeding through the wounds of these
stupid French people; I cry over their humiliations
and, however ungrateful and absurd they may be, I still
love them."

In contrast with most French literary men of the
time, Mérimée was truly cosmopolitan. He was a great
Anglophile; he spoke fluent English and was familiar
with the major works of English literature; moreover,
nearly every year he spent one or two months (late
spring, early summer) on the other side of the Chan-
nel – mostly in London, but also further afield, up to
Scotland even. (And, until his death, all his clothes
had to be cut by a Savile Row tailor.) He made repeated and prolonged visits to Spain (the country that
inspired his most popular novella, *Carmen*.[31] He was a
tireless traveller: Corsica (which inspired his *Colomba*),
Italy, Greece, Turkey, the Low Countries, Germany
… In the last part of his life, he applied himself to the
study of Russian and eventually undertook to translate Pushkin and his own friend Turgenev. Scholars
may find fault with these translations; still, they are
evidence of an uncommon intellectual energy and
curiosity.

Mérimée never married. His personal life was tumultuous and intensely busy, in contrast with his buttoned-up appearance as a proper gentleman. Decent people and notable conservatives (such as Guizot, for instance) who were aware of this other side to his life considered him, and his friend Beyle, as *polissons* (smutty scamps). He was a compulsive womaniser, netting a wide range of game, from prostitutes, minor actresses and young ballet-dancers to society bluestockings and duchesses. He also had great, and sometimes long-lasting, affairs of the heart. In this field he found much to share with Stendhal, "The man who fell in love as easily as other people would catch a common cold."

And finally – let us not forget – he was very fond of cats. He once boasted that he had owned one hundred and fifty cats (which seems a slight exaggeration; considering their average life-span, you would have to run a cat hostel to reach such a figure). As Baudelaire (another great cat-lover) remarked in a famous poem, cats are the favourite companions of "passionate lovers and austere scholars."[32] Mérimée certainly qualified on both counts.

APPENDIX II. *Note on Mérimée's* Henri Beyle

Mérimée had a long and close association with Henri Beyle and loved him dearly – but he did not really appreciate *Stendhal* and, in fact, hardly ever bothered to read him. This explains why his testimony is both priceless and cruelly limited.

At first, Mérimée had wished to write a brief portrait of his friend shortly after his death, but he realized how little he actually knew about him, and thus he tried to obtain some information from Romain Colomb, Beyle's cousin, who was utterly devoted to the deceased's memory. Mérimée's letter betrays an ignorance that is amazing as well as revealing: "I wish to write a few lines about poor Beyle, to be published in the [forthcoming issue of the] *Revue des Deux Mondes*. Could you provide me with some basic biographical data? Where was he born? Which positions did he occupy? I especially would like to mention the titles of his books and their dates of publication, at least approximately." Colomb, who himself intended to write such a memorial piece – for the same journal – simply ignored the request. (Colomb's article was eventually rejected.)

Eight years later, in 1850, Mérimée finally wrote this short, whimsical (and, in the eyes of some readers, shocking) portrait of his dead friend.

This text has a fairly convoluted history. Here it is, in simplified outline:

Mérimée wrote two different versions. The first one (1850) was privately printed by Mérimée himself in twenty-five copies, under the title of *H.B.*, and without any author or publisher identified. All personal names in the text were left blank – to be filled in by hand, by the author himself. Mérimée presented seventeen copies to intimate friends, common acquaintances and other connoisseurs (Delacroix, Sainte-Beuve, Romain Colomb, Viollet-le-Duc, among others) and he burned the rest (at least, that is what he said). The private distribution of this thin (twenty pages) anonymous pamphlet provoked intense curiosity and acquired a scandalous reputation; for quite a while Mérimée even denied being the author.[33] Very soon, several pirated editions appeared, under slightly different titles: *H.B.P.M.* and *H.B. par l'un des quarante* (*H.B. by one of the Forty* [members of the Académie Française]). The latter was issued in one hundred and forty luxury copies with, as illustration, an erotic engraving by Félicien Rops, printed in

Brussels, where there was a large industry specialising in the pirating of French books.

In 1855, Mérimée revised his earlier text and eventually used it as an introduction to an edition of Stendhal's correspondence. He corrected some errors, cut a few lines, filled in some details and – most importantly of all – considerably enlarged the overall contents of the piece.

A third and final version appeared posthumously (1874) under the title "Henri Beyle (Stendhal): Notes et souvenirs" in *Portraits historiques et littéraires*, a collection of Mérimée's essays and articles, written at different times (1826–1868), on Cervantes, Jacquemont, Brantôme, Froissart, Pushkin and Turgenev, among others; the editors of this volume reproduced the revised and enlarged version of 1855, preceded by the original 1850 version (with minor cuts).

Following the example of Jean Dutourd (see Bibliography), I chose to follow this third and longer version as it appears in *Portraits historiques et littéraires*. Though this text may lack formal perfection (the juxtaposition of two versions entails some repetition that would have offended Mérimée's stylistic perfectionism), its contents are richer and more accurate.

APPENDIX III: *Stendhal according to George Sand*

George Sand – pen-name of Aurore Dupin, Baroness Dudevant (1804–1876) – prolific and successful novelist, a good writer (though not a great one), was a remarkable woman: intelligent, generous, free and courageous; she was an early champion of women's rights.

Although married for some time, she eloped to Italy in December 1833 with a young lover, Alfred de Musset (1810–1857), a poet of genius and a feckless man. On the first leg of their journey, the lovers sailed down the Rhône, from Lyon to Avignon, by the regular steamboat. On board they met a fellow passenger, Henri Beyle, who was returning to his diplomatic post in Italy. George Sand had heard of him in the literary world, but this was her first – and only – encounter with the man himself. Some twenty years later, she recalled the experience in two pages of her autobiography, *Histoire de ma vie*. It is interesting to compare her fleeting impression with Mérimée's more intimate memories.

– A RIVER JOURNEY IN BEYLE'S COMPANY –
On the steamboat that was taking me from Lyon to Avignon, I met one of the most remarkable writers of

the time, Beyle, whose pen-name was Stendhal. He was consul in Civita Vecchia and was returning to his posting after a short stay in Paris. He had a brilliant mind; his conversation reminded me of Delatouche; it was not as tactful and elegant, but had more depth. At first glance, he looked a little like Delatouche too – fat, with originally delicate features, now grossly bloated; the latter, however, presented an occasional touch of beauty, whenever a sudden melancholy overcame him, whereas Beyle's mood was permanently sarcastic and bantering. I spent part of the day chatting with him, and found him most pleasant. He mocked my illusions about Italy and warned me that, very soon, I would have had enough of it; he said that the artists who went there in search of beauty were complete gulls. I did not lend much credence to this view; I realized that he was tired of his exile and was returning there with a heavy heart. In a very amusing way, he made fun of the Italian type, which he could not bear and towards which he was very unfair.[34] He forewarned me that I would suffer deprivation (which actually never materialized): lack of pleasant conversation and all that he considered as the aliment of intellectual life – books, magazines, news; in a word, current affairs. I fully understood what such a charming and original mind, with his entertaining mannerisms,[35] was missing when far away from a social circle that could appreciate and stimulate him. He displayed contempt for all vanities and tried to discover in each interlocutor some pretension that he could blast with his relentless gibes. But I do not believe he was a nasty man, although he tried hard to give such an appearance.

All his predictions regarding the boredom and intellectual emptiness of Italian life were exciting my interest rather than scaring me, since I was going there precisely to escape the sort of wit he imagined I was attracted to.

We had dinner with him and some other passengers in a mediocre village inn – the pilot of our steamboat did not dare pass under the bridge of Saint-Esprit before daybreak. He became jolly to a point of craziness; he drank too much and as he started to dance around the table in his thick fur boots, he was not a pretty sight.

In Avignon, he took us to visit the great church, located in a beautiful spot. In a corner, an old sculpture of Christ, a work of painted wood, life-size and truly hideous, provoked his fury; he exploded in incredible abuse. He hated these repellent realistic images, which, according to him, Southerners love for their barbaric ugliness and crude nudity. He actually wanted to hit this sculpture with his fists.

As for me, it was without regret that I saw the parting of our respective ways. Beyle was going to Genoa by land – he feared sea voyages[36] – whereas my intention was to reach Rome quickly. Thus we parted after having travelled together for a few enjoyable days. Still, since his mind seemed to betray a deep taste for obscenity[37] – it was his habit, or his dream – I confess I had had enough of his company; had he pursued his journey by sea, I might well have taken the mountain road. And yet he was an eminent man; on all things he had views that were penetrating, though unbalanced; his talent was original and true, but he wrote badly;[38] nevertheless he had a striking way of expressing himself and always captivated the interest of his readers.

PART II: Stendhal – *Les Privilèges*

INTRODUCTION

Les Privilèges was written in Rome, on 10 April 1840. Stendhal was once again very much in love at the time, but also in very poor health: he was to suffer a stroke the next year, and to die of another stroke the year after. A youthful impetus of passion combines here with intimations of old age and death, creating this strange, free flight into a world of imagination and dream. This extraordinary text – the purest example of Stendhal's compulsive confessional jottings – was never meant for publication.

This document, long neglected, was at last (in 1961!) given the attention and importance it deserves by the great Stendhalian scholar V. Del Litto, who pronounced it *"un texte capital pour la connaissance de Stendhal."*

Yet such a dashed-off, spontaneous style of writing, with its whimsical humour (quintessential Stendhalian flavour!), defeats the translator. Just consider the first word of the first sentence: *"God me donne le brevet suivant …"* How should one translate *God* into English?

THE PRIVILEGES

Stendhal

D EUS OMNIPOTENS grants me the following patent:

Article 1
Never any serious pain until a fairly advanced old age; and then no pain, but death by a stroke in bed, while asleep – without having to suffer any mental or physical distress.[39]

Every year, no more than three days of light illness. Body itself and all its discharges completely odourless.

Article 2
The following miracles will remain invisible and undetectable to all outsiders.

Article 3
The *mentula*:[†] like the index finger as regards hardness
and mobility, both qualities obtained at will. Shape:
two inches longer than the big toe, same thickness.
Pleasure from the *mentula*, however, will be enjoyed
only twice a week. Twenty times a year, the privileged
person shall be able to transform himself into whatever
creature he wishes, so long as that creature exists. One
hundred times a year, he shall be able to speak whatever
language he wishes.

Article 4
Miracle. The privileged person has a ring on his finger;
whenever he grips the ring while looking at a woman,
the woman will fall passionately in love with him,
the way we believe that Héloïse loved Abélard. When
the ring is slightly moistened with spittle, the woman
will merely turn into a tender and devoted friend. If
one takes the ring off the finger while looking at the
woman, the various feelings elicited in accordance
with the aforementioned privileges will cease at once.
Hatred turns into benevolence when looking at a
malevolent individual and rubbing the ring on the

[†]   Latin word for the male sexual organ.

finger. These miracles can take place only four times a year as regards passionate love, eight times for friendship, twenty times for the extinction of hatred, and fifty times for inspiring mere goodwill.

Article 5

Beautiful hair – splendid teeth – beautiful skin without the slightest blemish.[40] Body smell sweet and light. Every year, on 1 February and 1 June, the clothes of the privileged person are restored to the condition they presented the third time he was wearing them.

Article 6

Miracles. In the eyes of all those who do not know me, the privileged person shall present the appearance of General Debelle, who died in Saint-Domingue,[41] but without any imperfection. He will play an impeccable game of whist, écarté, billiards, chess, but shall never be allowed to win more than one hundred francs; he shall possess perfect skills at shooting, riding and fencing.[42]

Article 7

Miracle. Four times a year, he shall be able to transform himself into whatever animal he wishes to be, and afterwards revert to his original form. Four times a year, he shall be able to transform himself into any man of his choice; furthermore, he will concentrate his existence within that of an animal which, in the event of death or impeachment of number-one man (into whom he had transformed himself), shall be able, in turn, to bring him back to his own original human shape.[43] Therefore, the privileged person shall be able, four times a year and for an unlimited duration, to occupy two different bodies simultaneously.

Article 8

Whenever the privileged person shall carry, for two minutes, on his person or wear on his finger, a ring that he has briefly put in his mouth, he will remain invulnerable for whatever duration he determines. Ten times a year, he shall enjoy the sharp eyesight of an eagle and will be able to run a distance of five leagues within an hour.

Article 9

Every day at two in the morning, the privileged person shall find in his pocket one gold napoleon, plus the equivalent amount of forty francs in the currency of the country where he happens to be.[44] All the money that was stolen from the privileged person shall be returned the following night at two o'clock, on a table in front of him. Assassins, just as they are going to stab or to poison him, will be felled for eight days by an acute bout of cholera. The privileged person shall be able to abridge their suffering by saying: "I pray that the sufferings of So-and-so be stopped, or that they be changed into a less painful condition." Thieves will suffer an acute bout of cholera lasting for two days at the very instant they attempt their robbery.

Article 10

Eight times a year, when hunting, a little flag shall signal to the privileged person from a distance of one league the game that is hiding, and indicate its precise location. One second before the game starts to run, the little flag will become luminous – and of course, all along it will remain invisible to other people.

Article 11

A similar flag shall signal to the privileged person the location of statues hidden underground, under water and behind walls; he will be given information regarding their identification, their authors and potential market value. The privileged person shall be able to transform these statues into lead balls each weighing a quarter of an ounce. This double miracle of the flags and the transformation, successively, into lead balls and then back into statues, can take place only eight times a year.

Article 12

The animal that the privileged person rides, or which draws his carriage, will never be sick and will never stumble. The privileged person shall be able to communicate intimately with this animal, imparting his commands to it and sharing its feelings. Then, when riding a horse, the privileged person will become one with it, inspiring it with his will. In such a state of communion with the privileged person, the animal shall acquire a strength and power thrice as great as those it naturally possessed.

The privileged person, when transformed into a fly (for instance) and riding on an eagle, will become one with that eagle.

Article 13

The privileged person will remain incapable of committing any theft; if he attempts such a deed, his limbs will immediately fail him. He shall be allowed to kill ten human beings each year, provided these are people he has never spoken to. In the first year, he is allowed to kill one individual he has spoken to, provided this occurred on no more than two occasions.

Article 14
If the privileged person were to attempt to tell or disclose any one of these articles of privilege, his tongue shall be tied and become unable to form any sound, and he will suffer toothache for twenty-four hours.

Article 15
Within a radius of six metres from the finger-ring of the privileged person, all insects will instantly drop dead if the privileged person holding the ring says the following prayer: "I pray that all noxious insects may be annihilated." These insects include: fleas, bugs, all kinds of lice, crab lice, spiders, flies, rats, et cetera.

Snakes, vipers, lions, tigers, wolves and all venomous animals will run away in fright and remain at a distance of one league.

Article 16
Wherever he may be, the privileged person need only say, "I pray for my food," and he shall immediately

find: two pounds of bread, one beefsteak well-done, one leg of lamb well-done, one bottle of Saint-Julien,[45] one carafe of water, one fruit, one sorbet and one coffee. This prayer can be similarly answered twice in twenty-four hours.

Article 17

Ten times a year, the privileged person will hit whatever target he is aiming at, with gun, pistol or any other firearm.

Ten times a year, while fencing,[46] he shall display a strength twice superior to that of his opponent, whether in a duel or in a competition – but he will not be allowed to inflict a wound occasioning death, or pain and discomfort lasting more than one hundred hours.

Article 18

Ten times a year, the privileged person shall be able, by requesting it, to alleviate by three-quarters the suffering of any creature he encounters, or, if this creature is on the point of dying, he shall be able to prolong its life by ten days, while reducing its suffering by three-quarters. If he asks, he shall be able to obtain a painless and sudden death for this suffering creature.

Article 19

The privileged person shall be able to transform a dog into a woman, beautiful or ugly; this woman shall walk on his arm, she shall be as witty as Madam Ancilla and as tender as Mélanie.[47] This miracle can be repeated twenty times every year.

The privileged person shall be able to transform a dog into a man, who will have the countenance of Pépin de Bellisle and the wit of … (the Jewish doctor).[†]

Article 20

The privileged person shall never be more unhappy than he was from 1 August 1839 until 1 April 1840.[48]

Two hundred times a year, the privileged person shall be able to reduce his sleep to two hours, which will have the restorative effect of eight hours. His eyesight will be as sharp as that of a lynx; in his movements, he shall be as nimble as Deburau.[49]

Article 21

Twenty times a year, the privileged person shall be able to guess the inner thoughts of people around him, within a radius of twenty paces.

[†]   The identification is uncertain.

One hundred and twenty times, he shall be able to see what any person he thinks of is actually doing; there is, however, one absolute exception: the woman he loves most is not included here. Also excluded: all activities that are dirty or disgusting.

Article 22
The privileged person is not allowed to earn more than the sixty francs of his daily allowance by using the privileges listed here above.[50] One hundred and fifty times per year, he shall be able to ensure, simply by asking for it, that any individual whom he designates should forget him completely.

Article 23
Ten times a year, the privileged person will be transported to any place he wishes; he shall get there at a speed of one hundred leagues per hour; during the passage, he shall sleep.

BIBLIOGRAPHICAL NOTE

Needless to say, this little book is not a scholarly work. I made it for my own enjoyment and now, if I am publishing these pages, it is in the hope that they may also give pleasure "to the Happy Few".

Stendhalian studies fill entire libraries. I mention here only a few books which I personally found useful or stimulating.

Jonathan Keates, *Stendhal* (London 1994) is well researched and informative; it should satisfy Beylists, but may disappoint Stendhalians.

Jean Dutourd, *L'Âme sensible* (Paris 1959) is the exact opposite: it does not inform, it inspires. Written by a passionate lover of Stendhal's writings (Dutourd himself is a good novelist), it takes as its pretext Mérimée's little memoir, developing its every paragraph with pages of glosses. Free, whimsical, profound, paradoxical, sensitive, original – it is a treasure. I have kept re-reading it for half a century, and never tire of it.

Alain, *Stendhal* (Paris 1935, 1948): Alain is the pen-name of Alain Chartier, a remarkable professor of philosophy who taught generations of eminent French intellectuals, writers and thinkers (Simone Weil was his most brilliant student). Alain knew his Stendhal by heart; his comments are always original and thought-provoking.

Albert Thibaudet, *Stendhal* (Paris 1931): one of France's most perceptive literary critics reads Stendhal with lucid intelligence and sensitivity. (This book has been long out of print, which is a great shame.)

On Mérimée, quite a number of critical studies and biographies have appeared over the years. The latest one, Pierre Pellissier's *Prosper Mérimée* (Paris 2009), is a richly documented and well-written biography.

ENDNOTES

1   Auguste Sautelet (1800–1830), a 'bookseller' – as publishers
    were then called (he published one pamphlet by Stendhal) –
    and romantic dreamer with a somewhat confused mind.
    Stendhal mentioned him in a short note at the end of Chapter
    25 in *Vie de Henri Brulard*: "M. Sautelet, liberal publisher, blew
    his brains out around 1829 for reasons of vanity, love and debts."

2   Victor Jacquemont (1801–1832), naturalist and traveller, died
    prematurely of a tropical illness during a long and adven-
    turous expedition in India. He was eighteen years younger
    than Stendhal, but this age gap was no obstacle to their close
    friendship and mutual appreciation. With his brilliant talents,
    endearing eccentricities and abrupt sincerity, Jacquemont
    himself was very much the living incarnation of a Stendhal-
    ian character. Mérimée (who was also his friend) wrote a
    warm, perceptive and witty portrait of him in *Portraits his-
    toriques et littéraires* (the same volume that contains the ver-
    sion of *Henri Beyle* translated here).

    Stendhal himself evoked Jacquemont's memory in *Souve-
    nir d'égotisme*, Chapter 5, and in his correspondence.

3   Yet Stendhal strenuously opposed any attempt to introduce
    political opinions into a work of art. He repeatedly expressed
    this view (in *Racine et Shakespeare*, in *Armance*, in *Le Rouge
    et le noir*) with slight variations: "Any political idea in a work
    of art is like a pistol-shot in the middle of a concert. The noise
    is deafening and yet has no resonance."

4   "an utter aristocrat": this is confirmed everywhere in Stend-
    hal's writings – thus, for instance, this typical passage: "I had,

73

and still have, the most aristocratic tastes; I'd do anything for the happiness of the people, but I would rather, I think, spend a fortnight in gaol every month than live among shopkeepers." (*Vie de Henri Brulard*, Chapter 27)

5   A passionate and erudite Stendhalian, René Servoise, made a point which no one (it seems) had ever noticed before: the full title that Stendhal intended for his treatise *De l'Amour* (About Love) was in fact *De l'Amour, et des diverses phases de cette maladie* (About Love and the various stages of this illness). It is under this title that he himself listed it among his other books on the front page of the original edition of *La Chartreuse de Parme*. It is not without interest to know that Stendhal viewed love as a form of illness! (Proust would have approved.)

6   Actually, Stendhal's first great (yet unhappy) passion was inspired by Métilde Dembrowski. Madam C— is Countess Clémentine Curial. Stendhal fell in love with her in 1814 but only became her lover ten years later.

    "Général Caulaincourt was nearly as powerful as the Emperor. To get an idea of Beyle's daring, just imagine an obscure auxiliary employed in the Supplies Service of the Wehrmacht, who, in 1938, would challenge Goering to a duel." (J. Dutourd, *L'Âme sensible*, 42)

7   This is a famous verse from a satirical comedy by Jean-Baptiste Gresset (1709–1777).

8   On Stendhal's writing style and the incapacity of writers and critics of his time to appreciate it, see *infra*, Appendix III, George Sand's comment, and Note 38.

9   *Ibid*. George Sand had the same impression.

10 Actually, their first encounter took place in late 1821 or early 1822.

11 Mérimée was twenty years younger than Stendhal.

12 This is literally true – Mérimée was not prone to hyperbole.
The two men developed a deep mutual affection and, as much
as circumstances allowed, they became quite inseparable. In
the end, however, they subjected their friendship to a danger-
ous test: they travelled together (a long journey in southern
Italy in 1839); the two old bachelors, opinionated and irritable,
got on each other's nerves. Stendhal mocked Mérimée's obses-
sive desire to enter the Académie Française, and Mérimée
resented his sarcasm. Deeper down, however, though Stendhal
could accept literary criticism with unflappable serenity, he
must have been hurt by Mérimée's lack of interest in his writing. (What causes most distress to a writer is not negative criticism, but indifference.) The frictions of their journey brought
a marked cooling in their relationship, though it never reached
a point of estrangement.

13 Quote from Molière, *Le Misanthrope*.

14 Claude Adrien Helvétius (1715–1771), writer and philosopher
whose works Stendhal discovered with great enthusiasm as a
schoolboy. It is doubtful that he re-read him later in life
(though he mentions him in the early years of his *Journal*).

15 At the end of three of his books – *Promenades dans Rome* and
his two masterpieces, *Le Rouge et le noir* and *La Chartreuse de
Parme* – Stendhal (quoting from Shakespeare's *Henry V*, Act
4, Scene 3) inscribed the same words, in English:

TO THE HAPPY FEW

He often expressed the belief that he would find readers
after a hundred years (he could not have known how right he
was!). Meanwhile his readers were dismally few – a situation

75

that once provoked the jibe from his 'bookseller': "Your books are truly sacred: no one touches them!"

16 "maxims": Stendhal scattered them everywhere. In particular, he lavished them on his beloved young sister, Pauline (his letters to her form a thick volume): "Get used to sorrows; everyone experiences seven or eight of them each day"; "Never exaggerate the quality of a joy you do not have"; "Make good use of cold moments to improve your self-knowledge." Eugène Delacroix treasured a maxim that Beyle had designed especially for him: "Neglect nothing that can make you great." (Needless to say, 'greatness' for both of them had nothing to do with worldly success or social importance; it was purely an ethical and aesthetic notion.)

17 "tip for a first duel": Stendhal applied this method in his own very first duel, in which he engaged when still a schoolboy (age fourteen) against a huge and brutal school bully. He relates the episode with obvious pride and zest in *Vie de Henri Brulard*, Chapter 32.

18 The "small town" in question is Laon.

19 "stolen bliss": the woman whose name Stendhal "could not pronounce without keeping his voice from faltering" was Countess Clémentine Curial (see Note 6). When she ended their affair in 1826 (ten years before his confession in Laon), she caused him the cruellest sorrow of all his life.

20 "the lady": Angela Pietragrua, a "sublime whore, in the Italian style, in the style of Lucrezia Borgia."

21 On this subject, see *Vie de Henri Brulard*, Chapter 19: "If I had mentioned around 1795 my intention to become a writer, a sensible person might have told me: 'Write two hours every day, with or without genius.' With such advice, I could have

put to good use ten years of my life, which were wasted while I was stupidly waiting for genius."

22 Stendhal often expressed his hatred for bombast: "A ridiculous or merely exaggerated comment has often been enough to spoil the most beautiful things for me: for instance at Wagram, beside the gun, when the grass caught fire, that swaggering colonel, a friend of ours, who said, 'It's a battle between giants!' – the impression of grandeur was wiped out irremediably for that whole day." (*Vie de Henri Brulard*, Chapter 46).

23 On this subject, Stendhal could not have found a better teacher than Mérimée who, in his role as Inspecteur général des Monuments historiques, salvaged and restored countless architectural treasures, medieval cathedrals, monasteries and churches, which, without his enlightened and energetic intervention, would have disappeared forever.

24 Joachim Murat (1767–1815).

25 See *Mémoires d'un touriste*, entry Grenoble, 27 August [1837].

26 "entrance ticket": Jacquemont (see Note 2) gave a vivid account of Stendhal's talent as social entertainer. Newly returned from America and still in a state of disgust at the crass commercial vulgarity of that country, Jacquemont attended a *soirée* at which Stendhal was also a guest, and he marvelled at his friend's irrepressible verve: "Beyle was on form and honestly deserved that we should each give him ten francs for his effort, so amusing was he. Since I'd been deprived for a month of any form of wit comparable to his, I probably found him funnier still." Quoted in Jonathan Keates, *Stendhal* (London 1994), 320–21.

27 "Mr de M—": Baron Adolphe de Mareste (1784–1867) was for a very long time Stendhal's closest confidant and epistolary

alter ego – until 1836, when they quarrelled, having found themselves competing for the favours of the same mistress, "Madam Azur" (Alberthe de Rubempré).

28 An erudite Beylist calculated that, in his correspondence, Stendhal made use of some 350 different signatures, pen-names and false names, such as Le Chinois, Cornichon, Pardessus, Serviettes and Tonneau (respectively, The Chinaman, Gherkin, Overcoat, Napkins and Tub).

29 "the death he would have chosen": see *infra*, "The Privileges", Article 1 and Note 39.

30 Sophie de Beaulaincourt (who might have been one of Mérimée's countless lovers). Born in 1818, she was still alive at the end of the century, an impressive old lady. Proust visited her often, and it was with her image in mind that he created the character of Marchioness de Villeparisis (in *À l'Ombre des jeunes filles en fleurs* and *Le Côté de Guermantes*).

31 Bizet's opera remains hugely successful all over the world; yet both music and libretto are grossly inferior to Mérimée's stylish masterpiece. The writer's art was to be better served in the cinema: *Le Carosse d'or*, freely adapted by Jean Renoir from Mérimée's *Carosse du Saint-Sacrement*, is a classic of the screen (with the unforgettable Anna Magnani cast in the leading role).

32 *"Les amoureux fervents et les savants austères / Aiment également dans leur mûre saison / Les chats puissants et doux, orgueil de la maison, / Qui comme eux sont frileux et comme eux sédentaires."* (*Les Fleurs du mal*: Spleen et idéal, LXVI "Les Chats".)

33 To an English friend who had asked for a copy, he replied: "Ill-intentioned persons have attributed the authorship of this

pamphlet to me. Actually, it is an immoral piece of writing, which is evidence enough that it cannot be my work."

34 Stendhal had been madly in love with Italy – which he first discovered with enthusiasm, at age seventeen, as a cavalry officer in the victorious army of Bonaparte – but later he bitterly cursed the place and the people from the boredom of his consulate office of Civita Vecchia. After the Milan of his youth, where he had enjoyed an intoxicating atmosphere of liberation, he found in late middle age the provincial stuffiness of the Papal States a depressing anti-climax.

35 Stendhal's irrepressible exuberance often led people to believe that he was play-acting. George Sand, who met him for only three days, thought he was a poseur. This had also been Mérimée's first impression; but Mérimée came eventually to know him in depth, and realised that Stendhal was utterly true and sincere – absolutely incapable of any affectedness.

36 Stendhal suffered from sea-sickness. In his *Souvenirs d'égotisme* (Chapter 5) he noted that, if it were not for his fear of sea-sickness, he would gladly travel to America.

37 "a deep taste for obscenity": note that George Sand was certainly not prudish or prejudiced. She was a truly liberated woman, with a large circle of male friends – mostly writers and artists (Balzac, Sainte-Beuve, Flaubert, Delacroix) – and an equally large collection of lovers, the most famous of whom were Musset and Chopin; she even had an extremely brief affair – just out of curiosity – with Mérimée, but was not impressed by the experience and dumped him at once. (She notoriously told a friend, in confidence: "I had Mérimée the other night; it is not much.")

    Stendhal protected his sensitivity – and his vulnerability

– behind a veneer of contrived cynicism and schoolboyish bawdiness. This, in turn, could mislead not only superficial acquaintances but even – to some extent – as clever an interlocutor as George Sand.

38 "he wrote badly": nearly all contemporary writers made this same comment. Of course, George Sand was not exactly the best judge of this subject; but a man like Mérimée, who was an outstanding stylist, ought certainly to have known better. Yet even he could write (at the time of Stendhal's return from Italy, autumn 1833): "Our age has left Beyle far behind. He no longer understands the fine nuances of our French language, and has not yet learned the new idiom with which we have enriched it during his absence."

At the time of Stendhal's death, Victor Hugo concluded: "Mr Stendhal will not reach posterity, because he never had the faintest inkling of what writing is."

And even Balzac, who wrote the only glowing review of *La Chartreuse de Parme* (he found it "sublime"), still felt the need to add one reservation: "the weak side of the book is its style."

39 Romain Colomb (cousin of Stendhal) noted on the copy he made of the original manuscript of *Les Privilèges*: "Whenever Beyle was talking about death, he expressed the wish to have his life ended by a stroke, in bed, while asleep, during a journey, in a village inn. This wish, often repeated, was answered at least as regards its principal object on 22 March 1842."

Stendhal, age fifty-nine, was felled by a stroke on the pavement of a street in Paris (rue Neuve-des-Capucines). He was carried home to rue Neuve-des-Petits-Champs, where he died later in the night, without pain and without having regained consciousness.

A year before, he had noted: "I find that there is nothing ridiculous about dropping dead in the street, so long as one does not do it on purpose."

40 Stendhal had a desperate need to love and to be loved, which made him all the more painfully conscious of his own awkward and unattractive appearance: short, fat and balding (he wore a toupee), he thought he had "the facies of an Italian butcher."

41 General Jean-François Joseph Debelle (1767–1802) was famous for his physical beauty; he died during the military expedition that Bonaparte sent to Saint-Domingue.

42 Stendhal's clumsiness at fencing was for him a source of much distress – he was too fat and too quickly out of breath – but it never discouraged his pugnacity. He used to compensate for his lack of skill with reckless impetuosity. (On this subject, see *Vie de Henri Brulard*, Chapter 42.)

43 The syntax of this sentence is garbled in the original.

44 Towards money, Stendhal had a splendid detachment, which reflected another aristocratic aspect of his character. Writing about Delacroix, who shared that same attitude, Baudelaire quoted him: "Stendhal said that a sensitive man must endeavour to secure the minimum necessary for his independence; once such security is obtained, to waste time in increasing one's wealth would be abject." (Charles Baudelaire, *L'Oeuvre et la vie d'Eugène Delacroix*, 1863, viii. Actually, Baudelaire developed here an observation that Stendhal had made in *De l'Amour*, II, "Fragments divers," 61. On this same subject, see also *Vie de Henri Brulard*, Chapter 46.)

45 "Saint-Julien": a red Bordeaux wine, produced in southern Médoc and still popular today.

46 On fencing, see Article 6 and Note 42.

47 "Madam Ancilla": Madam Ancelot (1792–1875), a literary lady whose *salon* was much attended by Stendhal in the late 1820s. In her book of reminiscences, *Les Salons de Paris* (1858), she drew this perceptive sketch: "Beyle was excited by everything and went through a thousand different sensations in a few minutes. Nothing escaped him, nothing left him cold, but his sorrows were hidden under jesting and he never seemed as happy as when expressing the liveliest contradictions." (Quoted in Jonathan Keates, *Stendhal*, London 1994, 309)

   "Mélanie": Mélanie Guilbert, nicknamed Louason (1780–1828), a young actress whom Stendhal met in 1804. He went to live with her in Marseille for nearly two years, then got bored: "the earliest fully realized liaison of Stendhal's life, and one of the very few in which his passion was adequately recompensed." (Keates, *ibid.*, 82)

48 This extreme misery was probably related in some way to two events: he met an early love again (Giulia Rinieri) and he developed the last passion of his life (Countess Cini?). The allusion remains obscure.

49 Deburau was a famous mime and funambulist of the Romantic era.

50 See Note 44.

ACKNOWLEDGMENT

This little book did greatly benefit from the judicious suggestions and careful editing of Adam Shaw, to whom I wish to express here my very special gratitude.

S.L.